ABOUT MY GRANDMA:

This Is Grandma

Her name: _____

How I call her _____

Her age: _____

Our favorite thing to do together is

....

....

Grandma And Me Drawing

I love hearing stories about

....

....

LOVE HUG SPOIL

This is what

GRANDMA

Is all about

I love you because you tell me I am

....

....

MY GRANDMA IS

AW _ SO _ E

I love it when we play

....

....

I love the way you give the best
advice when

....

....

I love you because
when I feel sick, you always

....

....

I love you because you make the best

....

....

MOMMY
knows a lot
but GRANDMA
knows everything

I love that you taught me

....

....

This is Grandma in three words:

My favorite place in your house is

....

....

You are so funny when

....

....

You deserve the

....

....

Award

I will always cherish that day when

....

....

A picture of us:

I love you because you can

....

....

faster than anyone

I love you because you can fix

....

....

I drew this picture for you, Grandma

I love you because
you make the yummiest

....

....

My favorite place to go with you is

....

....

Grandma, you make the good moments better and the hard ones * easier

I feel most loved when you

....

....

I would definitely like to do this

with you again

If you were a color, you'd be

....

....

Draw Grandma's favorite flower

The most amazing thing we have done together is

....

....

I know you are the happiest when

....

....

This is Grandma

By Me

I love the way you cheer when I

....

....

This is Me

By Me

You are very good at

....

....

Together we make the absolute best

....

....

TEAM

When we are apart, it makes me happy to think about

....

....

I Love You,
GRANDMA
You Are
The Best

I know you love me because

....

....

"I love you more than all the frosting on a cupcake, Grandma!"

The most important thing I learned from you is

....

....

I am really grateful for

....

....

"Every day is special when I get to spend it with my Grandma."

You are the best
Grandma ever because

....

....

Want FREEBIES?

Email Us At:

larasvows@gmail.com

Title the email "What I Love About Grandma For Kids" and let us know that you purchased our book.

THANKS FOR YOUR AMAZING SUPPORT!

>>>>>>>>>>>>>>>>>>>>>>>>>>>>

For Enquiries and Customer Service
email us at:

larasvows@gmail.com

We don't exist without you. A brief review could help us a lot. Please leave your feedback about this book.

SCAN THE OR CODE BELLOW

>>>>>>>>>>>>>>>>>>>>>>>>>>>>>>>>>

THANKS FOR YOUR AMAZING SUPPORT!

Made in United States
Orlando, FL
09 May 2023